CALM AF

AF

Laid-Back Advice for Getting the
Better of Anxiety, Coping with Stress
and Staying Chilled Every Day

SAM BAXTER

CALM AF

An Hachette UK Company
www.hachette.co.uk

Vie Books, an imprint of Summersdale Publishers Ltd
Part of Octopus Publishing Group Limited
Carmelite House
50 Victoria Embankment
LONDON
EC4Y 0DZ
UK

www.summersdale.com

Printed and bound in China

ISBN: 978-1-78783-542-9

Substantial discounts on bulk quantities of Summersdale books are available to corporations, professional associations and other organizations. For details contact general enquiries: telephone: +44 (0) 1243 771107 or email: enquiries@summersdale.com.

DISCLAIMER
The author and the publisher cannot accept responsibility for any misuse or misunderstanding of any information contained herein, or any loss, damage or injury, be it health, financial or otherwise, suffered by any individual or group acting upon or relying on information contained herein. None of the views or suggestions in this book is intended to replace medical opinion from a doctor who is familiar with your particular circumstances. If you have concerns about your health, please seek professional advice.

CONTENTS

INTRODUCTION

It's not easy being cool, calm and collected. Life can be great – hello stuffed crust! – but it can also be a big, ugly pile of stress that you can't avoid, no matter how strong your anti-anxiety air freshener is (or how much pizza you order).

   If you want to be chill, then you've come to the right place. With this bible of calm, you'll learn how to mellow your mind in any situation and how to fight off everyday unease with, well, ease. While you're at it, you'll also discover all the secrets to transforming your home into a place where you can kick back and relax, as well as tips on keeping your worries at bay when you're out, about, and living your #bestlife.

Before we get into it, let's keep it real for one second: you're not a superhero with magical mind-altering powers (unfortunately), so doubts *are* going to creep in and try to screw with your mood from time to time. But remember that everybody has bad days sometimes, even Beyoncé. Simply by employing some of the following advice, you'll be on the road to feeling calm AF in any situation.

You can't calm the storm, so stop trying. What you can do is calm yourself. The storm will pass.

TIMBER HAWKEYE

WHY AREN'T
WE CALM AF?

Our prehistoric ancestors didn't have mindfulness, and they seemed to cope just fine. Then again, they didn't have social media, delayed trains, or rent to pay either, so by comparison keeping calm for them was a Palaeolithic breeze. These days, we've got at least 99 problems, and stress is definitely one of them. The causes are many and varied: overflowing inboxes, Instagram insecurities, the climate crisis, money problems... The list could go on, but it won't. Instead, here are some simple tips to help you handle those everyday stressors.

MEET UP WITH YOUR MENTAL HEALTH

To quote an Ancient Greek affirmation: know thyself. This motto is just one of the great ideas that the Greeks had (including philosophy, the Olympics, maps and democracy) and it should probably be considered the first commandment of good mental health.

In order to know thyself, pay attention to the way that you feel. Remember: your emotions are not static. They change from day to day, and sometimes hour to hour, often without warning. They can be influenced by outside forces (work stress, financial problems, friend drama), they can relate to past experiences or ongoing trauma, or they can change for no discernible reason at all. Confusing? Yes. Normal? Also yes! Some people have a lot of ups and downs, and that's OK. Others don't have as many, and that's OK too. Pay attention to your mind to get familiar with your own tendencies, because when you know thyself, you're more easily able to help thyself.

STRESSED SPELLED BACKWARDS IS DESSERTS.

LORETTA LAROCHE

WHEN THE WALLS
ARE CLOSING
IN, JUST STEP
OUTSIDE AND
TAKE A BREATH.

DON'T PLAY THE BLAME GAME

Once you've accepted that not every day is not going to be like an episode from your favourite nineties sitcom, it's time to point the finger and blame yourself for this pile of chaos called your life, right? WRONG. In fact, you couldn't be more wrong. Expectation is one tough mother, because she has a real habit of leaving you disappointed and, as a result, way more stressed. Whether you're down because your plans haven't turned out as you wanted, or because you're not feeling the way you want to, don't sweat it, and definitely don't beat yourself up about it. The way to feel better is through treating yourself with kindness and forgiveness.

EMBRACE THE
GLORIOUS
MESS THAT
YOU ARE.

ELIZABETH GILBERT

STRESS: THE TRASH CAN OF CRAP

If calm is a baby unicorn leaping gaily from cloud to cloud, stress is a giant trash can of crap that empties itself all over the floor when you've just tidied up: messy, unwelcome, and difficult to deal with. The reason it's difficult to deal with is because the contents of the trash can are debilitating: raised blood pressure, a flood of stress hormones, shallow breathing, physical pain and a lack of sleep to name but a few. These are all things that make it harder for you to face the things you're stressed about. Hello cycle from hell.

If you're not sure if you're stressed out, watch out for behaviour changes, which could indicate that stress has got its trash-covered claws into you. Are you losing your temper easily? Are you reaching for food or alcohol more than usual? Are you unable to sleep, or concentrate at work? Don't be afraid to ask others if they've noticed anything different too.

Long-term stress can be damaging to your health, so if you've been experiencing these feelings for a while, don't be afraid to seek professional help.

When life gives you lemons, make whatever lemony treat you damn well please.

CALM AF IN THE BODY

Your body might not literally be a temple, but you should certainly respect it like it is. From the food you eat to the dance shapes you throw, a healthy bod feeds into a healthy mind from which true serenity can emerge. Whether you're reaching for another glass of wine or unable to peel yourself off the couch, take these tips on board to know when your physical choices are getting in the way of your emotional well-being, and then give them a good ol' shake-up.

GET A VITAMIN FIX

It's important to keep your body stocked up with the good stuff for optimum energy, nutrition and general all-round good vibes. B vitamins are super important when it comes to regulating your mood because they help the body produce serotonin, a neurotransmitter that helps you feel good. Supplements are available, but they're also found in whole grains, dark green leafy veg, beans, peanuts, eggs, and avocados.

Vitamin D also boosts your serotonin levels, and you can get this for free. Yay, free stuff! The sun doesn't need to be out for you to feel the effects, but if it is, slap on some sunscreen and get out and about. If you're cooped up inside for most of the day, getting your vitamin D fix is even more crucial. Schedule outdoor breaks during the day to soak it up, because your mood can be boosted whether you're sitting still or strolling.

(And don't forget, always seek advice from your doctor when significantly changing your diet or taking supplements.)

Take care of your body.
It's the only place you
have to live.

JIM ROHN

I AM THE
CALM
BEFORE,
DURING AND
AFTER THE
STORM.

SAY HELLO TO HOMEMADE

There's a reason it's called comfort food – the clue's in the title. And when we're feeling low, there's nothing like a big bowl of something delicious to soothe the soul and the belly. But rather than piling your plate with takeout and processed food, which will probably leave you feeling sluggish, unleash your inner Michelin-star chef and whip up your favourite comforting dish. Homemade curries, chillies, stews and soups are packed with wholesome veggies and spices to nourish your body, and you'll feel so much better knowing you made it all from scratch.

FANCY A TEA?

I'd love one, please! Always say yes to a cup of tea – caffeine-free if you prefer. According to actual science, drinking tea has a similar effect on the brain as meditation. So when you're holding on to a hot cuppa, slowly sipping away, you're also stimulating alpha brainwaves that are associated with relaxation and mental clarity. Take it to the next level of chill with a soothing camomile, especially in the evening, which is ideal for relaxing your muscles and reducing stress. Tea-tastic!

ALMOST EVERYTHING
WILL WORK AGAIN
IF YOU UNPLUG IT
FOR A FEW MINUTES,
INCLUDING
YOU.

ANNE LAMOTT

HYDRATION ELATION

People shout about the benefits of plain old water, but getting those six to eight glasses of the good stuff each day really can make you feel awesome. Water intake helps make sure your brain is functioning on full power, so you can concentrate, and keeps your mood in check, staving off anxiety and sleepiness. (Water allegedly blesses you with glowing skin too. We can't guarantee you'll experience this side effect, but bonus points if you do.) Sick of plain H_2O? Chuck in a few mint leaves, slices of cucumber or citrus fruit for a splash of excitement.

HUG IT OUT

The "cuddle hormone" is possibly the cutest
kind of hormone science nerds have ever
named. Oxytocin, to give it its formal moniker,
is released when we hug, touch or sit close
to someone else. In women especially it
causes a reduction in blood pressure and
the stress hormone norepinephrine. So,
if you're feeling uptight and out of sorts,
grab your buddy and get cuddling for a
hormone hit that will give you all the feels.

SNACK A LITTLE SMARTER

You might have heard of stress eating – the realization usually hits when you're four glazed donuts down – but what about stress hunger? When your blood sugar levels are low, any stress or anxiety you're feeling is going to be amplified because your body might be releasing extra adrenaline to keep you going. In turn, this will make you feel even more anxious – it's a vicious cycle! Balance out your blood with a naturally sugary snack, like fruit, and follow it up with a high-protein snack, such as a handful of almonds, to avoid crashing when the sugars wear off. Sip water and take care of your tummy. The butterflies are real, man!

Take
a walk
on the
wild side...
or just
to the
park.

LET'S PUMP IT UP

Squats might give you tight buns, but the science shows that working out also does wonders for your mental health – doctors even recommend it for helping with depression. The reason? Happy hormones (endorphins) are released when you get in a sweat, with the bonus of making you feel confident and capable, too. It can be hard to get started, so begin with something you can handle: a walk each day, a jogging app for beginners, a fun aerobics class, a cycle to work, or a dip in the pool. Most importantly, pick something you enjoy, and get chasing those endorphins!

Stop a minute, right where you are. Relax your shoulders, shake your head and spine like a dog shaking off cold water. Tell that imperious voice in your head to be still.

BARBARA KINGSOLVER

Be your own cheerleader (with or without the pom-poms).

GET SOME ZZZs

Sleep is not just that thing you do when you're not looking at your phone. It's a vital process your body goes through every day – without it, your attention span, emotional responses, and memory will suffer, and you also put yourself at higher risk of heart disease and high blood pressure. We need roughly eight hours of sleep each night, but everyone is different, so figure out what works for you.

Getting to sleep is usually half the battle. To help, put a bedtime routine in place, just like you would for a tiny, innocent child: turn off electronic devices, take a warm bath, drink a decaffeinated hot drink, put on cosy pyjamas, and then read a book or meditate to relax your mind. Try not to get into bed too early, and only turn the lights off when you feel sleepy – don't lie there in the dark if you're wide awake. More top tips for optimum sleep include: a room temperature of 16–18°C (60–65°F), darkness (think blackout blinds or eye masks), a comfortable mattress and pillow, and no loud noises. If you live in a noisy area or have sh*t housemates, try using some earplugs.

FEELIN' THE HEALIN'

Alternative therapies might not be your bag, but hear this out. Many people claim that reiki is a great way to relieve tension from your body. For those not up on their energy healing practices, reiki involves the transfer of universal energy from the practitioner's palms to your body (either by holding their hands over you or through touch). While not scientifically proven, many celebs swear by its healing and relaxing properties. If you're still not sold on this idea, try a deep-tissue massage instead to soothe physical pain and release tension.

I LONG FOR THE
COUNTRYSIDE.
THAT'S WHERE I
GET MY CALM AND
TRANQUILLITY –
FROM BEING ABLE
TO COME AND
FIND A SPOT OF
GREEN.

EMILIA CLARKE

PANIC PROBLEMS

Most things about stress aren't particularly fun, but panic attacks come pretty high up on the list of Things That Suck. These devils are an abrupt and intense rush of fear where you might experience a racing heart, shallow breath, trembling, sweating and chest pain. Good times! You might even feel paralyzed and fixed to the spot. If you're prone to panic attacks, remember they are not physically dangerous however frightening they feel. Next time the panic monster is paying you an unwelcome visit, breathe as slowly and deeply as you can. You've got this.

A STEADY
BREATH, EVEN
BEFORE YOU'VE
BRUSHED YOUR
TEETH, CAN
CALM A
TORNADO
OF TERRIBLE
THOUGHTS.

STRIKE A POSE

Yoga isn't just for bendy Californian types in booty shorts and sports bras. Originating in ancient India, it's a physical, mental and spiritual practice that comes in many forms. In the West, a lot of yoga schools practise a form of Hatha yoga, made up of a series of poses. By regularly performing these poses, you can improve your core strength, flexibility and posture as well as reducing your stress, increasing your energy levels, and improving your concentration. Heck yeah.

If you're worried that you don't have the right body for yoga, then ask yourself the following question: do you have a body? If the answer is "yes" then you have the right kind of body!

To get started, find out about the classes in your area, or check out video tutorials online. Once you know what you're doing, you can do a daily practice at home or keep attending classes for further guidance. You could even mix up physical yoga with spiritual meditation for even more calming results. However, if the yoga revolution is not calling to you, some deep static stretches every day in the style of a lazy house cat will feel pretty darn good too.

Step outside for a while
– calm your mind. It is
better to hug a tree
than to bang your
head against a
wall continually.

RASHEED OGUNLARU

FABULOUS FATS

Sure, kale is good, but your body also needs essential fatty acids (EFAs) – good fats – to stay fuelled up and feeling good. Our bodies don't produce them, so you've gotta go out and eat them yourself. Stock up on omega-3 by chowing down on oily fish (salmon and mackerel), avocados, nuts, olives (hello, tapas!), olive oil, chia seeds and flaxseeds. Remember, trans fats, the kind you find in most processed foods, are still unhealthy in large quantities, so, unfortunately, this isn't an excuse to eat an entire cheeseboard.

STOP TRYING TO MAKE EVERYONE HAPPY. YOU'RE NOT A JAR OF NUTELLA.

YOU BOOZE, YOU LOSE

Sometimes a glass of wine is exactly what you want to help you chill out, unwind, and enjoy the end of the week. And there's nothing wrong with that. But if you feel like you *need* that drink (or other drug of choice), maybe that's not such a good thing. With sobriety becoming more common, even among the cool kids, you can cut down on the booze or ditch it completely without getting serious FOMO. What they tell you in school is true: drugs impact your mental health, and dependency can lead to problems that will kill your inner calm.

A BREATH
OF FRESH AIR

Remember when you were a kid and you were about to do something nerve-wracking and your mum or the teacher would say, "Take a few deep breaths"? Well, turns out they were pretty smart. Whether you're preparing for a stressful life event or just feeling overwhelmed, sitting in a relaxed pose and taking a few minutes to breathe deeply can really help to calm you down in the moment. And that's because science is doing its thing: long breaths trigger neurons in your brain that tell your body to relax.

Try breathing in through your nose and counting slowly to four in your head and out through your mouth to a count of five. You might think you're a busy bee with no time to sit around breathing, but that's where you're wrong! You can do this anywhere and everywhere – on the bus, at your desk, before you hop in the shower, just before bed – for one minute or five, or even more. And if sitting quietly counting to yourself isn't your thing, take your deep breathing out into the world. Go for a walk, preferably somewhere green, and suck in the oxygen-rich air that Mother Nature has to offer.

BREATH IS THE
POWER BEHIND
ALL THINGS. I BREATHE
IN AND KNOW THAT
GOOD THINGS
WILL HAPPEN.

TAO PORCHON-LYNCH

Be a pineapple: stand tall, wear a cute crown, and be sweet on the inside.

KATHERINE GASKIN

DANCE YOUR GLOOM AWAY

Letting go and breaking free by throwing some killer shapes on the dance floor always feels so good, but did you know that you can do this even when you're *not* in the club at 2 a.m? Wherever you are and whenever you need it (whether you're alone, with friends, in public, etc.), turn on the tunes that make you want to move, because dancing helps you to get rid of tension – plus it triggers the release of endorphins to make you feel great. If you want a regular dance sesh, you could join a class to keep your spirits high. If your two left feet give you anxiety, an online dance workout video means you can get all the pleasure with none of the embarrassment.

WHY BE MOODY WHEN YOU CAN SHAKE YOUR BOOTY?

EVERY DAY
BRINGS A
CHANCE FOR
YOU TO DRAW
IN A BREATH,
KICK OFF
YOUR SHOES,
AND DANCE.

OPRAH WINFREY

CALM AF IN THE MIND

If you thought "mindfulness" was an annoying buzzword that they throw around on daytime TV and during workplace wellness seminars, you'd be right. But it isn't just that. Taking time out every day to check in with yourself, to ask "How am I feeling?", is really important. Life is stressful, and even if it looks like you're doing fine on the outside, you might be really struggling on the inside. Be your mind's ally, rather than its enemy, by taking up some of the tips in this chapter.

THE WRITE STUFF

Words can be overwhelming (just think of your inbox after you've been away on holiday), but they can also be super useful. Writing things down is a simple but effective way to hush those hassling thoughts and restore order. What are you waiting for, Shakespeare? Pick up your quill (or use your phone) and get scribing to calm yourself down:

- **To-do lists:** from work tasks to shopping lists to your Chinese takeaway order, a list stops you from having to store all that info in your brain, giving you more headspace for the things that really matter.

- **Journalling:** get those feels out of your head and down onto paper. A notebook filled with your thoughts, fears, and wishes is a great way to put your worries to one side, or to work through any problems you're facing.
- **Letters:** Catch up with someone the old-fashioned way. Unlike texts and email, letter-writing requires actual time and thought, allowing you to think about how you feel without the pressure of the other person's immediate response. A letter gives your thoughts space to breathe (and the gesture is cute AF too).

SMILE, BREATHE AND GO SLOWLY.

THÍCH NHẤT HẠNH

WHEN YOU
HOLD GRUDGES,
YOUR HANDS
AREN'T FREE TO
EAT COOKIES.

SINGING FOR THE SOUL

You don't need to be Ariana Grande to belt out a tune (although it does help). When we sing, we feel A-MAZING because endorphins – happy hormones – are released in our beautiful brains. Singers are found to have lower cortisol levels, too, which is a good indicator of less stress. So, pick your favourite playlist and sing along in the shower, in the car or anywhere else that takes your fancy (maybe not the library, though). To go one step further, join a choir or get your friends together for karaoke. When we sing with others, oxytocin also puts in an appearance, which means you feel a greater sense of bonding and community in the process. So sing-sing – it's win-win!

FULL-BODY CALM

We don't only feel anxiety in our minds – it gets into our bodies too. So, next time you feel stressed, try persuading your body to relax, because sometimes your brain will follow too. Lie down on your back and close your eyes. On an inhale, tense your toes as hard as you can for five seconds. As you exhale, release the tension until they're limp again. Repeat this all the way up your body – with your feet, your legs, your butt, your tummy, your arms, hands, shoulders (you get the idea) – until you're done, and see how much more relaxed you feel.

Our greatest defence
against stress is the
ability to change our
minds; to change
our thinking.

GOLDIE HAWN

LIFE IS BETTER WHEN YOU'RE LAUGHING.

SAY YES TO *PONO*

Forgiving and forgetting is damn hard, but holding a grudge or hating yourself is going to kill your calm like nothing else. For some people, saying sorry and accepting apologies comes easily, but if you're struggling to forgive, try the Hawaiian forgiveness process, *ho'oponopono*, which literally means to become doubly *pono* (*pono* is a state of feeling calm and at peace with a situation or person).

1. Don't just tell someone you're over it – tell a person you forgive them and then ask for their forgiveness too. This makes the process more involved and committed.

2. Talk it out. Tell your side of the story and allow the other person to tell theirs too. You don't have to agree, but you have to both feel heard. When you're done, tell them you've said everything you want to say on the matter.

3. Feel the love by trying your hardest to feel compassion towards the person who's wronged you (and yourself). Chances are, a misunderstanding or unsettled disagreement from the past has caused the issue. This will help you to move past this moment together.

4. Pain is a pain in the ass, but it's also part of life. Learn what you can from this tricky situation while letting go of the negative emotions associated with it.

GET THE
INSIDE RIGHT.
THE OUTSIDE
WILL FALL
INTO PLACE.

ECKHART TOLLE

WRITE IT OUT

You are powerful, capable and awesome, and some days *you know it*. But there will always be the days when you're not feeling those vibes so strongly. On these kinds of days, pushing your worries to the back of your mind and hoping they'll just go away is tempting – but resist! We've been there before, and take it from us: those worries aren't going anywhere. You need to face them – and if you need somewhere to start, writing them down can help. Look at your worries objectively. What steps could you take to overcome them? Do you need to tell someone? Would professional advice help? Seeing your fears as real, surmountable parts of your life makes them much easier to address.

When I
woke up
this morning,
I had no
plans to be
awesome.
But, hey,
sh*t happens.

BREAK THE CYCLE

We've all been there. You're lying in bed, or going about your day, and the same negative, self-sabotaging, distracting thoughts keep looping in your mind like a bad sitcom that's always on repeat. Rude. When this happens, you need to break the cycle. Focus on one positive thing that's happened to you this week, and hold onto this. Then think of another, and then another. If this doesn't work for you, imagine that your negative thoughts are something a friend is saying about themselves. How would you respond to them? Whatever you do, the aim is to break the loop of your thoughts by actively thinking or doing something different.

YOU'RE ON
A BEACH...

Unfortunately, most of us can't swan off to the beach and chill out whenever we feel like it. We have work to do, bills to pay, people to see – all that everyday jazz. That's why being able to visualize yourself someplace soothing is a great skill to have, particularly at times when the stress is high. Your happy place might be a tropical beach, a serene snowscape, your favourite coffee shop, or even your bed. Once you know what makes you mellow, try out the following technique.

Close your eyes and keep them closed. Take a few deep, slow breaths. Picture your happy place and start to notice things in your imaginary idyll. We mean *really* notice things, like sounds, scents, tastes and textures. What's the temperature – baking sunshine or chilled autumnal goodness? Are those waves? Are they lapping? Is that your duvet, so soft and so snuggly? Relax all your limbs. Then, when you feel soothed, open your eyes. You won't have magicked yourself to a five-star spa, but you might at least feel like you've been to one.

The better people
are at taking care of
themselves, the more
effective they'll be in
taking care of others.

ARIANNA HUFFINGTON

**Some days
I amaze
myself.
Other days
I leave my
keys in the
fridge.**

MAP YOUR MOOD

To stake your claim to the calm crown like a Miss Universe winner (minus the fake tan and tears), you must learn to identify what winds you up and brings you down. Do you freak out in big crowds, talking to strangers, or being the centre of attention? Maybe you stress when specific subjects come up or perhaps noise, lighting, air quality, and temperature have an impact on how you feel? Knowing exactly what makes you stressed is the first step to owning your stress, managing it and potentially overcoming it.

SHINY, HAPPY PEOPLE

For some people, being and remaining positive comes easily, but for most, it is HARD WORK. Instead of grabbing one of these positive people by the lapels and yelling at them to tell you their secrets, you can try this instead. Whenever you experience something good – the taste of your morning coffee, the compliments you get on your new outfit, the satisfaction of finishing a good book – take the time to really notice it. Make other people aware of it too and comment out loud if you want! If you do this enough, looking on the bright side will start to become a habit, and before long, there'll be too many good moments to possibly comment on them all.

A DAY WITHOUT WITHOUT SUNSHINE IS LIKE, YOU KNOW, NIGHT.

STEVE MARTIN

DON'T LET IDIOTS RUIN YOUR DAY.

MEDITATION STATION

Modern life is full of distractions. You might feel like you're doing something productive when you're checking Twitter and swiping through your Tinder matches, but generally you're just keeping your mind from focusing on other things. Meditation can help you with this – allowing you to achieve that golden duo of both calm *and* focus. There are a whole bunch of different meditation techniques you can try – you might be focusing on your breath, your body or a chant – but ultimately, meditation is about clearing your mind.

Here's a simple meditation exercise. Sit in a comfortable position (use cushions to help support your weight) and relax your body by taking a few slow, deep breaths. When you start out, it might be hard to keep that focus, but if your mind starts to think about what you're going to eat for dinner or what your ex posted on Facebook, simply bring your thoughts back to the present and continue. Aim for a ten-minute meditation session per day to start with – maybe when you get up or straight before bed – and build the time up slowly. Try a meditation app or a class first if you're feeling a bit daunted about flying solo.

Meditation is like
having a phone
charger for your
whole body
and mind.

JERRY SEINFELD

CREATIVE CONTROL

Whether you're artistically challenged or the world's next Picasso, spending some time getting arty and crafty is a great way to unwind and focus on something other than your worries. Art as therapy is nothing new and we all know it can do wonders for your mental health – but you don't actually need to pay a professional to enjoy it. The great thing about being creative is the one golden rule: that there *are no rules*. It's more about the doing than the result. Whether you're drawing, painting, sculpting, knitting, sewing, baking or making a mural out of dried pasta and glitter glue, just make sure you go for it and let your creative juices flow (beret optional).

**Note to self:
I'm going to
make you
so proud.**

NO SPOILERS!

If binge-watching any half-way decent TV show has taught you anything, it's that good stories are full of surprises. In life, those personal plot twists can be joyful and terrifying, but they're also what keep it interesting. And like any good show, even though you might want to know what's going to happen, if you found out ahead of time, you'd be PISSED OFF. By embracing the unknown in your own life, and getting comfortable with the fact you're never going to know what's round the corner, you can let go of the anxiety that goes along with uncertainty. Your show finale is a long way off, so take life one episode at a time, and you'll enjoy the series so much more.

THANK YOU VERY MUCH

Gratitude ain't no platitude! If your manners are on point, you probably say "thanks" multiple times every day: to that beardy bro who makes your latte; to your buddy for buying you a drink; to the neighbour who received your Amazon order because you were out galivanting... But did you know that being thankful for all the pluses in your life is also a top technique for cultivating optimism? That's right. It's been scientifically proven that gratitude can increase happiness, boost energy, improve sleep, promote kindness and enhance spiritually. Oh yeah, all the good stuff.

When people are kind, take the time to truly thank them. And when good things happen, make sure you acknowledge the gratitude you feel. If you want to hold onto these sweet feels, a great way to do this is with a gratitude journal. At the end of each day, write down one or two things that you're grateful for that day. It could be how good your sandwich was, how much you enjoyed your workout, or how awesome your friend is. When you're feeling low, read through these entries to help remind yourself of all the amazing things in your life.

THINK BIG THOUGHTS
BUT RELISH SMALL
PLEASURES.

H. JACKSON BROWN JR

FAKE IT TILL YOU MAKE IT

You've heard the phrase "You've got to fake it to make it" – it may sound silly, but it's true. Research suggests that even a forced, fake smile (like the kind you find on retail employees when you walk into the shop five minutes before closing time) can decrease your stress levels and brighten your mood. Next time you feel less than fine, dredge up some pretend inner sunshine and smile. Keep it up and pretty soon you won't be pretending any more. Why? Cos you got this.

LIFE MAY
GIVE YOU
A CACTUS,
BUT YOU
DON'T
HAVE TO
SIT ON IT.

YOU ARE NOT YOUR THOUGHTS

You probably know your outer voice really well (that's the one making small talk with the Uber driver and asking everyone what they're eating for lunch), but what about your inner voice? This one is a harder nut to crack – narrating silently, worrying about things that you needn't worry about. When your inner voice has turned up the volume on those anxiety-ridden thoughts, don't be afraid to take a step back and acknowledge it. Really stare it out. Hear what it's saying and remember that thoughts are just thoughts. They come from you, but they are not who you are and, if they are bringing you down, you don't have to listen to them.

THEY'LL BE THERE FOR YOU

If you're the kind of person who likes everyone to think you're doing just fine – even when you're so far from fine that fine is a tiny pigeon on the horizon that you can barely identify as a pigeon – then you need a reality check. Your good friends love hearing about your highs, but they also want to be there to support you during your lows. Don't be afraid to send a message or make a call to someone who cares about you, even if it's just to say you've had a crappy day. If they're worth keeping in your life, they won't think any less of you for sharing your vulnerabilities. If anything, they'll love you even more.

CALM AF
AT HOME

Home is where the heart is, but it's also the epicentre for some of our main causes of stress. If you can't remember the last time you saw your bedroom floor, you're forever fire-fighting your bank balance or you never feel like you can properly relax at home, this chapter is for you, as it addresses some of the key stress hotspots in the home and how to handle them.

URBAN JUNGLE

Bringing some of the outside into your abode has a whole load of benefits for your mental and physical health. House plants don't just brighten the place up and make your home look like a trendy coffee house (although that's certainly a big part of what they do). Thanks to photosynthesis, plants also increase oxygen levels in the air, which is particularly great for city-dwelling humans. Orchids and succulents keep releasing oxygen through the night, so they're ideal for your bedroom. Plants are good news for those of us who suffer from dry skin, colds and sore throats too, because they increase the moisture in the air, helping to tackle these ailments.

Studies have even shown that being surrounded by plants boosts concentration, memory and productivity – wonderful if you're working from home and great for your general mental well-being.

If you love plants but hate the way they always die on you, then look for a low-maintenance species. There are plenty of them, and they're just crying out for a spot in your home. Shop around, seek out advice, and start small with one or two plants. Then, as your green-fingered flair builds, so can your urban jungle.

When I look at myself in the mirror, I see a badass who's gonna get stuff done.

YOUR BEDROOM IS YOUR BEST ROOM

If you share a house with friends or family, your bedroom is the place you go to ~~escape~~ relax. Be sure you've got all the storage you need to maximize floor space (mount cupboards on the walls and put drawers under the bed) so that you have room to use the space as you please, whether that's for watching TV, doing a spot of yoga, or entertaining sexy guests. Make your bed every day too, so it always looks inviting in the evening (also a good idea in case of aforementioned sexy guests). Finally, decorate with all the patterns, colours and trinkets that you love to make the space well and truly your own.

I hate housework.
You make the beds,
you wash the dishes
and six months later
you have to start
all over again.

JOAN RIVERS

SLAY YOUR LIFE ADMIN

Like a kick-ass group of superheroes, we all have our own strengths. For some, it's dealing with life admin and for others its binge-watching three seasons of one TV show in a day. If you don't fall into the former group, then stop burying your head (and your paperwork) in the sand and admit that this is something you might need help with. Ask your friends, family or a professional assistant for help with managing your bills, money and other important administrative tasks. Believe it or not, some people are seriously into this stuff and are champing at the bit for you to ask. Once they've helped you set up a system that works, you'll find the whole adulting thing a lot more manageable.

GOOD BATCH!

Batch cooking is not just for burly gym types who are protein-packing and carb-loading. It's also a great way to get organized for the week ahead so you can worry about more important things, like choosing a killer outfit for the day or remembering to bring your keys with you when you leave the house. Sunday afternoon is a great time to plan, prep and make your meals, whether you're preparing breakfast pots, lunches, big dinners or all three. Here are some top tips:

- Make sure you have a good quantity and variety of containers for the different types of dishes you're going to prepare.

- Slightly undercook veggies so when you reheat them, they're not overdone.
- Try reusable freezer bags instead of boxes to fit more in your fridge/ freezer.
- Label everything neatly so you always know what you've got and when you cooked it.
- Make batches of sauce for things like pasta, so all you need to do is cook the pasta and then heat up the sauce.

WE'RE
ALL LIKE
CHAMPAGNE:
BEST WHEN
CHILLED.

FLIP THE
OFF SWITCH

You're not alone – we're all drawn to the glow of our phone screens like moths to a flame. But we should be wary, as, for all social media's positive aspects, there are just as many negatives. There is mounting evidence that using these apps can contribute to anxiety, depression and higher stress levels. One of the reasons for this is because the more time we're looking at our screens, the less time we're interacting with our fellow humans, and less IRL facetime means increased anxiety and feelings of isolation. Use timer apps to limit how long you're spending on certain addictive apps (oh the irony!) and for a calmer, more fulfilling home life, step away from that phone.

FOR A LIST OF
ALL THE WAYS
TECHNOLOGY HAS
FAILED TO IMPROVE
THE QUALITY OF
LIFE, PLEASE
PRESS THREE.

ALICE KAHN

NAP TIME

You may think that naps are the domain of infants and the elderly, but that's where you're wrong. Naps are the human equivalent of turning something off and on again to make it work. All you need is 20 to 30 minutes of sleep in the afternoon, and this can be the restorative solution you need lift your mood, increase your alertness, or prepare you for that night out you have planned. If you need a nap regularly, the chances are you're not getting good enough quality sleep or you're pushing your body too hard, but an occasional half hour of shut-eye to give yourself a boost is an invaluable power move for people with places to go and people to see.

I make no secret of
the fact that I would
rather lie on a sofa
than sweep beneath it.

SHIRLEY CONRAN

Tidy
home,
tidy
mind.

CUT THE CLUTTER

We've all got a cupboard, a drawer, or even a whole room filled with crap that we can't bear to face – a dumping ground, or household purgatory, where possessions, papers and odd bits and pieces are discarded because there's nowhere else to put them. Now, possessions themselves are perfectly acceptable – but when their presence starts to have power over you, making your life stressful and unmanageable, that's when you need to start sorting.

There are a number of different approaches you can take to clearing out the clutter from your home: sorting room by room; spending ten minutes decluttering per day; or sorting through possessions by type, as suggested by Japanese professional tidier Marie Kondo.

However you choose to tackle your scary cupboard/drawer/room, throwing things out with intention, knowing that you no longer need or want them, is the key. It's important to feel free to get rid of objects that no longer bring positivity into your life – photos of people you don't like anymore, clothes that don't fit, books that you never plan on reading... With all these things out of the way, your home will feel spacious and inviting, rather than panic-inducing.

THE BEST
WAY TO FIND
OUT WHAT WE
REALLY NEED
IS TO GET
RID OF WHAT
WE DON'T.

MARIE KONDO

HOW CAN
YOU CHANGE
YOUR LIFE IF
YOU HAVEN'T
EVEN DONE
THE DISHES?

KEEP IT CLEAN

A clean home is a calm home, so by
maintaining a hygienic and tidy space, you're
doing your physical and mental health a
huge favour. Don't worry about living up
to unrealistic standards or try to keep your
house so clean that you could eat your
food off any surface. Nobody's got time for
that. Instead, to keep things manageable,
assign days of the week to tackle different
jobs. That way you're ticking things off
on a regular basis. And, if you live with
others then share the load! Make sure your
housemates or family are pitching in too.

SWEET-SMELLING THERAPY

If you love the smell of calm in the morning (and maybe in the afternoon and evening too) then try aromatherapy, which is self-care via your nose. It's long been believed that the smells of essential oils affect the hypothalamus, the part of the brain that controls the glands and hormones, thereby changing a person's mood and lowering their stress levels. To try this fragrant therapy for yourself, add a few drops of essential oil onto a tissue and inhale, or add a few drops to your bath in the evening. Some relaxing scents include chamomile, lavender and rose, and refreshing oils include black pepper, peppermint and rosemary. However, if you are using essential oils for the first time it is advisable to consult your doctor first.

YOU CAN DO ANYTHING, BUT NOT EVERYTHING.

DAVID ALLEN

I can't always live in the moment, so I moved in next door.

SAVING UP FOR SUNSHINE

They say you should save for a rainy day, but you don't have to be feeling blue to enjoy yourself. Rather than blow your bucks every payday, save a little bit each week towards something you're super excited about: concert tickets, a fancy dinner out, a weekend away... Having a positive goal and a deadline to save for (rather than a rainy-day pot that you never spend) will motivate you to stay on track. Banking apps are often a great way of keeping tabs on your spending and helping you to save for the next sunny splurge.

If you're working towards a big financial goal, like buying a car or saving for a house deposit, and sacrificing lots along the way, it can be slow-going and dispiriting. Build mini-treats into your saving schedule, e.g. When I've saved £500, I am going to get my nails done, or when I've saved £1,000, I'm going to enjoy a big night out with my friends. It will make the long haul a lot more bearable, and allow you to track your progress in a much more interesting way.

ON TOP OF THE CHORES

A looming list of must-dos, need-to-happens, and gotta-sorts is beyond choresome. From everyday tasks to big home improvements, knowing these things are lurking in the corners of your home can make being there unbearable. But you probably know from experience that once you get started, things rarely take as long as you think they're going to. It's just the getting going that's the hard part.

Write a list of all the tasks that need to be accomplished – breaking them down by how long you estimate each task taking (you can also arrange them according to urgency, i.e. clean the bathroom, STAT). Assign tasks to evenings and weekends over the next month. Imagining yourself organizing a filing cabinet in one evening is a lot less stressful when you see it as a standalone chore, rather than alongside fixing the kitchen tap, organizing a friend's hen-do, filling in job applications, doing the weekly shop, etc. And remember, some things are achieved more efficiently with a little help from your friends (or qualified professionals). Don't be afraid to ask for help or pay for it if you can.

If your compassion does
not include yourself,
it is incomplete.

JACK KORNFIELD

YOU BELIEVED IN
SANTA CLAUS FOR
SEVEN YEARS – SO
YOU CAN BELIEVE
IN YOURSELF FOR
FIVE MINUTES.

DATE YOURSELF

Having a busy social calendar is brilliant, but it's important that you take the time to look after number one too. Being alone has a bad reputation, but it doesn't have to be lonely and sad; it's a way to recharge, regroup, to check in with yourself about how you're feeling... and because it's just you, you can do whatever the heck you want! If you need a few ideas, try going for a meal out on your own or a trip to the movies, or simply going for a stroll. Even better: schedule this time into your week like a date so you won't feel that you're missing out on being with others.

SOAK IT UP

The bathroom shouldn't just be the spot where you wash, brush and go. Some relaxing tub time can make a world of difference after a particularly stressful day. Every bathroom can be a spa if it tries hard enough. Light scented candles to fill the room with cosy light and a soothing fragrance, put on some relaxing music, and use bath salts or essential oils in the water to relieve aches and pains and moisturize your skin. If you're not the bathing type, opt for a long, hot shower instead.

**Life is
like a bath:
the longer
you're in it,
the more
wrinkled
you get.**

If you think nobody
cares if you're alive,
try missing a couple
of car payments.

EARL WILSON

HOW ABOUT A HOBBY?

Remember when you were a kid and you'd have a packed schedule, filled with making, doing, exploring, and screeching really loudly before inexplicably peeing yourself? You were so busy enjoying life and trying new things that your adorable little brain probably didn't have time to question your place in the universe. Now you're stuck in a loop, shuttling yourself from work to home and back to work again, it's much easier to get in a funk and feel blue.

Thinking deeply is important, but don't forget to get out there and enjoy all that life has to offer. If you already have a hobby, great! Dedicate time to it every week, especially if it's something you can do with others. The commitment will make you feel connected to a wider community, not to mention you'll probably improve (Karate black belt? Yes please!) and start to notice the benefits. If you're currently hobby-less, try out a bunch of new classes, meet-ups and activities to see what works for you and then pick something that you really enjoy. Having pursuits outside of work, home and family commitments will add a new joyful element to your life and give you something to work toward.

WARDROBE WIN

One of the most difficult parts of the day is deciding what to wear, so make life easier – and so much calmer – for yourself by organizing your wardrobe. Donate the things that you don't wear, throw out the things that are old and worn. One easy trick to find out what you do and don't wear is to turn all your hangers so they face the opposite way round to usual. As you wear things over the next few months, take stock of the hangers that stay untouched. Instead of scratching your head trying to remember the last time you wore those trousers, the wardrobe will answer this question for you.

CALM AF IN THE WIDER WORLD

So you've got yourself sorted in your mind and body (yes, you are looking HOT), and your house is the zenith of Zen. But what about when you step outside into the big, bad world? There's work stress, holiday stress, and don't forget about sitting on a sweaty bus in rush hour (oh the horror). Keep your wits about you, and follow these simple tips to make sure both your inner and outer self remain calm AF.

MINDFULNESS ON THE GO

So, you've got this far through the book and now you know exactly how to calm yourself down after a tough day, and you've got plenty of things in your schedule designed to keep you feeling zen. But what about when you're out and about? It's as difficult as it sounds to get out your yoga mat for a quick downward dog on a packed commuter train, so if you feel anxious and your options are limited, try some mindfulness on the go.

Pick any object in your surroundings and concentrate on its shape and texture in order to block out other distractions: it could be your bag, a rock on the ground or the graffiti on the seat in front of you, for example. Allow everything else to zone out around you while you look at your object and notice all the tiny details – textures, shapes, scuff marks, shadows. Focusing intently on one object keeps your mind from wandering over to other places, and gives you a chance to unwind from whatever tension you are experiencing.

STOP
WORRYING
ABOUT THE
POTHOLES IN
THE ROAD
AND ENJOY
THE JOURNEY.

A SHIP IN
HARBOUR
IS SAFE,
BUT THAT
IS NOT WHAT
SHIPS ARE
BUILT FOR.

JOHN A. SHEDD

EVERYBODY CRIES

If you need to cry, then let it out! It's often our gut reaction to try to hold tears back, but crying is a healthy and perfectly natural reaction. As well as being a way to release stress and tension, it means that you're acknowledging and confronting your feelings instead of bottling them up and pushing them away. Tears also help to cleanse the body of the chemicals that raise cortisol, the stress hormone. So, if you're particularly stressed and feel the urge to cry, that's your body's way of trying to make you feel better. Find a quiet space (or don't) and let it all out until you feel ready to face the world again.

KEEP YOUR FEELINGS YOUR OWN

If dealing with your own stress and anxiety wasn't hard enough, spending long periods with other people means you might encounter a dose of theirs too – whether it's at work, on a trip, or with family for the holidays. Be the voice of reason by making sure everyone's opinions are heard (including your own), be prepared to compromise (do you really need the last Brussels sprout?) and know that it's OK to take a break when you've had enough – that's what a quiet corner and the latest binge-worthy series is for.

STRESS
DOES
NOT GO
WITH MY
OUTFIT.

IN THE END
YOU WON'T
REMEMBER THE
TIME YOU SPEND
IN THE OFFICE
OR MOWING
THE LAWN.
CLIMB THAT
MOUNTAIN.

ANONYMOUS

TAKE TO THE TREES

Sure, the cabin-in-the-woods lifestyle ain't for you – hot showers, Netflix and microwaved snacks are much too sacred for that. But that doesn't mean you can't partake in the Japanese practice of *Shinrin-yoku*, which translates as "forest bathing". No, you don't need to cut up some twigs to join you in the tub. Instead, take yourself off to a spot of woodland, and immerse your mind and body in the space. Whether you're sitting on a stump staring up at the canopy or strolling slowly through the trees, being among these leafy entities will reduce your stress levels, lower your blood pressure and boost your mood.

While you're at it, kick off your shoes and socks and try "earthing". Ever wondered why it feels so good to go barefoot at the beach? Being shoeless in nature helps you to connect with the natural world. Visualize your stress melting away through your toes into the ground. Try this in your garden, at the park on your lunch break, or when you're out and about at the weekend.

LIVE YOUR BEST LIFE

If you feel stuck in a rut, don't be afraid to mix it up a bit. Take up a new hobby, try something that scares you, meet people with different perspectives, and travel somewhere you've never been (even if it's as simple as getting off at the next bus stop). When your natural inclination is to say, "I wouldn't enjoy that" when faced with an activity you just haven't tried, or "I'm busy" when you're planning on re-watching all 236 episodes of *Friends* for the fourth time, it's probably a good idea to embrace the unknown and all the wonder that lies in wait.

ALWAYS BE PREPARED

As eco-friendly as it is, public transport should really be outlawed. Whether it's a bus, train or even plane, all those sweaty bodies shoved in together sharing germ-infested air is enough to send even the most calm and collected people into a state of elbow-digging, seat-stealing hysteria. While you can't control the timetable or ticket prices, you can control the snacks, stuff and entertainment you bring to "enjoy" the ride. Whether it's an eye mask and ear plugs, the latest episode of your favourite show, comfortable clothes, a bottle of ~~wine~~ water, crossword puzzles or even some stinky food to annoy your fellow travellers, the choice is yours.

THIS TOO
SHALL PASS.
IT MIGHT
PASS LIKE
A KIDNEY
STONE, BUT
IT WILL PASS.

Security is mostly a
superstition. It does
not exist in nature.

HELEN KELLER

THE POWER OF "NO"

Although we've spent some time extolling the virtues of saying "yes", it's equally (if not more!) important to appreciate the power and value of its opposite: "no".

Our days can quickly fill up with the things that we agree to do for other people; it's easy to feel that you have to do what's asked of you, to please others, to meet expectations or to maintain a reputation. But the negative effects of taking on more than you should are manifold, including – you guessed it – that it's gonna put your stress levels through the roof.

Next time you're asked to do an extra job, whether it's at work or at home, assess your schedule and decide whether you want to take it on, whether you have time to, and what effect it's going to have on you. Don't be afraid to say "no" if you need to. It can often be the healthiest choice, because you need to have the energy to look after yourself before you can help others. It can be hard at first – as we're conditioned to be people-pleasers – but once you get the hang of it there'll be no stopping you.

WATCH MORE SUNSETS THAN NETFLIX.

THE BEST
WAY TO
APPRECIATE
YOUR JOB IS
TO IMAGINE
YOURSELF
WITHOUT
ONE.

OSCAR WILDE

BRAVE NEW WORLD

Going somewhere new – whether it's a new job, a different country, or even just a new café – can be genuinely scary, like those freaky twins in *The Shining* scary. There are lots of things that can go wrong, sure, but there are also lots of things that probably won't. Don't let your fear of the unknown hold you back. Get as much information in advance as you can to allay your fears, and keep your wits about you as you go. Trust your gut instincts and you'll be fine. You can't control the world around you, so stop trying and start enjoying everything it has to offer.

PLAN TO RELAX

Holidays are usually a time where you intend to kick back and relax, but when you enter the planning stages and see all the incredible things your destination has to offer, it can be tempting to try to fit everything in all at once. While this might give you some bumper Instagram content, it certainly won't be relaxing, because your holiday turns into one mammoth to-do list. To avoid this problem, start by telling yourself that it's not physically possibly to see and experience every single thing. Make the most of what you encounter and leave room for relaxation and spontaneity, or don't book anything in advance and just see where the mood takes you.

Sometimes the most scenic routes are the detours you didn't mean to take.

DON'T WORRY
ABOUT THE
WORLD ENDING
TODAY. IT'S
ALREADY
TOMORROW IN
AUSTRALIA.

ANONYMOUS

Airplane travel is nature's way of making you look like your passport photo.

AL GORE

AWAY FROM IT ALL

If your normal schedule is as chaotic as a
Black Friday sale, going on a trip probably
doesn't faze you, but for the more rigorously
routined, a change from the norm is pretty
panic-inducing. Fight off those freak-outs
by writing a checklist of everything you need
to do before you leave. Make arrangements
with a trusted friend or neighbour to take
care of your house, plants, furry friends,
etc., and remember: when you're away,
try to keep your mind on all the fun you're
having, rather than fixating on the fact you
probably (definitely) didn't leave the oven on.

CRUSH WORK WORRIES

Grown-up life is HARD. And work is a big part of that. Bad bosses, long hours, crappy pay... there's lots to complain about (that's what ~~Monday, Wednesday and~~ Friday drinks are for!). Don't let your overwhelming workload grind you down – talk to your manager, even if you don't get on, and set realistic targets; celebrate the little successes, like "job well done" emails (and not getting too drunk at the Christmas party); and recognize your human-ness. You're not going to be perfect all of the time (especially when there's an open bar at the Christmas party).

CHANGE YOUR THOUGHTS AND YOU CHANGE YOUR WORLD.

NORMAN VINCENT PEALE

DON'T WORRY,
BETTER DAYS
ARE COMING.
THEY ARE CALLED
FRIDAY, SATURDAY
AND SUNDAY.

BALANCING ACT

Work/life balance is definitely something dreamed up by self-made millionaires who spend most of the year lounging on super yachts with Hollywood types. But that doesn't mean you shouldn't shoot for the stars and try to incorporate it into your own life. Take as many breaks throughout the day as you can get away with. Use up all your holiday days, even if it's just to lounge around at home in your pants. Try to leave on time and, above all, make sure that your life is not your work. Enjoy time with friends, explore new interests, and for god's sake, turn your email alerts off. There's nothing so important it can't wait until the morning.

FIND SUPPORT AT WORK

No one is an island – we all need a bit of support. Unfortunately, workplaces can be severely lacking in this department. That's why it's up to you make sure you have access to the help you need. Find out if your work has an employee assistance programme in place – these will offer free advice and counselling. Get to know your Human Resources contact (or your trade union if you have one), and don't forget to take the time to get to know your colleagues too. Join them for lunch or suggest grabbing a coffee, because they will be your biggest allies and support if things get tough.

VOLUNTARILY CALM

Whether you're caught up in a whirlwind of worry or as chilled as they come, it's easy to put your own thoughts and worries first. But did you know doing something for others is one of the best ways you can improve your own mental health and well-being – did someone say, "two for the price of one!"? Try volunteering for a local organization, raising money for a good cause, mentoring a young person or throwing out random acts of kindness whenever the mood takes you (the lattes are on you!). In return, you should experience reduced stress levels, a sense of belonging, a renewed perspective on your own problems, and a longer life expectancy (thank you very much!).

ASK THE EXPERTS

You wouldn't fix your own car (unless you're a mechanic, in which case, you got this!) or plumb your own toilet (shout-out to all the plumbers!), but when it comes to handling mental health issues, there's an assumption that we should be able to handle it all ourselves. Sometimes a bit of professional help is the only thing that will do. Asking for it is often the hardest part, but once you've reached out, you'll find there are lots of options for managing stress, anxiety and depression with someone else's help.

Here are just a few:

- Talking therapies, like counselling, cognitive behavioural therapy and life coaching, give you the chance to discuss your feelings in depth without worrying about burdening a buddy. With trained professionals, you can work through your past, and look to the future.
- Try aromatherapy, reiki, or massage to relax your body so you can find calm in your mind.
- Hypnotherapy can help silence negative thought patterns and change your behaviour, or have a go at art therapy to examine underlying psychological and emotional disruptions.

CONCLUSION

It's inevitable that there will be days when you don't feel so calm. Yep, some days are just gonna suck. Hard. But that doesn't mean you can't flex your mindfulness muscles and, using all the tips this book has to offer, emerge relatively unscathed on the other side.

Calmness is the prize, and your eyes are firmly fixed on it. You now know how to mellow your mind, take care of your body, stress-proof your living space, and avoid the panicky pitfalls of life in the wider world.

You can recognize that your mental health is a bit like riding an 18-speed mountain bike – there will be ups, downs, and everything in between. And that's OK, because the tools in this book are your gear levers and brakes, and you are firmly in control.

After all this reading, you have everything you need to go onward and live your calmest and happiest life. You're officially a peacefulness pro, which means, in other words, you're calm AF, and you got this.

RESOURCES

Because you're smart and know that asking for help is a sign of ultimate strength, you may find the following useful if you're in the UK:

The Samaritans: a 24-hour free, confidential helpline to support you whatever you're going through. samaritans.org; 116 123; jo@samaritans.org / jo@samaritans.ie

Mind: support and advice to help empower anyone experiencing a mental health problem. mind.org.uk

StepChange: providing advice for handling debt. 0800 138 1111; www.stepchange.org.

Drinkline: the UK's free, confidential national alcohol helpline.
0300 123 1110 (open weekdays 9 a.m. to 8 p.m.; weekends 11 a.m. to 4 p.m.)

For readers in the United States:

Mental Health America: promoting the overall mental health of all Americans. mentalhealthamerica.net

National Institute of Mental Health: the lead federal agency for research on mental disorders. nimh.nih.gov; 1-866-615-6464

National Suicide Prevention Lifeline: free, confidential support for people in distress. suicidepreventionlifeline.org; 1-800-273-8255

MINDFULNESS AND MENTAL HEALTH APPS

What's Up?: uses cognitive behavioural therapy techniques to help you cope with depression, anxiety, stress, anger and more

Mind Shift: great for young adults with anxiety, this app acts as a little cheerleader in your pocket.

Happify: this psychologist-approved mood-training programme includes engaging games, gratitude prompts, and activity suggestions to help you overcome negative thoughts.

Headspace: one of the most popular mindfulness apps on the market, headspace helps you to incorporate mindfulness and meditation into your daily routine.

Calm: guided meditations, sleep stories, relaxing music... what more could you want from an app designed to help you overcome moments of stress and anxiety?

If you're interested in finding out more about our books, find us on Facebook at Summersdale Publishers and follow us on Twitter at @Summersdale.

www.summersdale.com